AMISH COOKING

CLB 2378
© 1989 Colour Library Books Ltd., Godalming, Surrey, England
All photographs of Amish life © 1987 by Blair Seitz
All rights reserved
This 1993 edition published by Crescent Books,
distributed by Outlet Book Company, Inc., a Random House Company,
40 Engelhard Avenue, Avenel, New Jersey 07001
Printed and bound in Italy
ISBN 0 517 68911 1
7 6 5 4 3 2 1

AMISH COOKING

CRESCENT BOOKS
NEW YORK • AVENEL, NEW JERSEY

INTRODUCTION

In 1727 a small band of religious people arrived in Pennsylvania from Germany. Strict and devout, they called themselves the Amish after their leader, Bishop Jacob Ammann. Divided by their beliefs, both secular and religious, from other European communities in the sixteenth and seventeenth centuries, the Amish had migrated from Switzerland to Alsace and then to Germany, before settling finally in North America.

The Amish have always lived their lives as models to simplicity, honesty and harmony. Even today, the old ways are still deemed the best. Transport is by horse and buggy, and horses still pull the plows. New buildings, whether houses or barns, are built by communal effort. There is no electricity, so light comes from propane lamps, stoves and refrigerators use bottled gas, and rooms are heated by wood-burning stoves or open fires. Small wonder that families gravitate to the warmth of the kitchen when the day's work is done.

This simplicity also extends to the Amish diet. Food is wholesome and nourishing, plentiful, but not extravagant. Although most of the land is devoted to growing grain and corn, each Amish farm has a large kitchen garden full of fruit and vegetables. Some of this produce is put up in traditional glass storage jars by the Amish women so that it is available for them to use throughout the winter.

The foundation of Amish cooking is in the recipes the people brought with them, and these are mainly Germanic in origin. As Amish settlements grew in both the United States and Canada, their recipes were shared and so now they offer a real clue to the Amish way of life all over North America. Theirs is a wholesome, hard-working philosophy which harks back to the pioneer spirit.

As in any family-oriented society, meals are very important to the Amish, and a typical Amish day always leaves time for cooking and baking. Bread dough is set to rise before the washing commences, and bakes while the clothes are hung out to dry. After some housework, sewing or work in the kitchen garden, it's time to start the midday meal, or dinner: a filling stew perhaps, with fresh or canned vegetables according to the season. After dinner, the women might make cakes, quick breads or pies, helping with the planting or milking while they bake. Finally thoughts turn to supper, the main meal of the day, when everyone is sure to be at home. It might be spareribs with sauerkraut or a savory meatloaf with potatoes, and there is always room for dessert.

Despite their simple, hard-working life style, Amish people still enjoy plenty of social occasions – opportunities to get together and share recipes. On Sundays, they often take it in turns to hold services in their homes and, after the service, everyone stays to dinner, often bringing a contribution to the meal. Chicken and dumplings or baked chicken with its crispy coating are Sunday dinner favorites, accompanied perhaps by broccoli with sauce and succotash and cornmeal rolls or biscuits. An array of desserts follows, since Amish women are accomplished bakers. Shoo-fly Pie is a well-known Amish dessert and pies of all sorts are very popular. Cakes, such as chocolate angel food, are also considered the perfect ending to a meal.

Another very popular social occasion for Amish women is the quilting bee, a time for them to exchange both ideas and recipes. Everyone stays for supper, of course, and a casserole is a good answer when a quick, easy and tasty meal is needed.

A communal house building or barn raising is also a good excuse for cooking and baking. Each of the families involved brings a contribution to the meal, and there are always hearty main dishes plus a colorful selection of gelatin salads, pickles, relishes and preserves, home-baked breads and candies to keep the children happy. Plates are filled with delicious home-made fare and after giving thanks, everyone is admonished in true Amish fashion to "Clean your plates empty!"

Just one word of advice before you begin trying out these delicious recipes. The number of servings is not specified and, in true Amish style, the quantities are often very generous. After all, you never know who may drop by and need feeding! Keep this in mind and be sure to adjust the recipes to your own requirements where necessary.

Onion Tomato Soup

Ingredients

4 tablespoons margarine
½ medium-sized onion, cut up
Celery leaves, dried or fresh
½ cup flour (approximate)
Tomato juice (about 4 cups)

Water
Sugar
Salt
Red pepper or paprika
Cream or milk

Sauté in the margarine the onion and some celery leaves. When the onion is tender, stir in the flour until it is slightly browned, then slowly add tomato juice. Stir the mixture to smooth the lumps until it becomes the thickness of gravy. Add some water, sugar, salt and red pepper or paprika to suit your taste. Before serving this soup add some cream or milk.

Above: when tobacco is ready for cutting, able-bodied members of all generations help to get it in.

Split Pea Soup

Ingredients

1 cup dried split peas
3 quarts water
1 ham bone
1 tablespoon minced onion
3 tablespoons butter

3 tablespoons flour
1 teaspoon salt
Pepper
2 cups milk

Soak the peas overnight in water, drain them in the morning and cover them with 3 quarts of water. Add the ham bone and onion and cook them until they are soft. Melt the butter and stir in the flour until they are well blended and smooth. Add the salt, some pepper and the milk and cook, stirring constantly until the mixture thickens. Combine it with the peas and ham bone and cook it until the soup is rather thick.

Above: this beautiful quilt is being sold at a benefit auction for one of the community organizations on which the Amish depend.

Succotash Chowder

Ingredients

1 large onion, chopped
3 tablespoons butter
1 cup fresh or canned corn
1 cup fresh or canned lima beans
2 cups potatoes, diced
1 cup water
1 teaspoon salt
¼ teaspoon pepper
3 cups milk
2 tablespoons flour
¼ cup water
1 teaspoon parsley, chopped

Sauté the onion in the butter in a pressure cooker until the onion is slightly browned. Add the vegetables, 1 cup of water, and the salt and pepper, cover, and set the control. After the control jiggles, cook the mixture for 2 minutes, then reduce the pressure immediately. Add the milk and heat it to boiling. Blend the flour with the water to make a smooth paste, and add it to the soup, cooking it for 1 minute while stirring constantly. Garnish the servings with chopped parsley.

Above: feeding the calves is a good introduction to farm animals for small children.

Winter Vegetable Soup

Ingredients

1 pint celery	1 pint corn
1 pint carrots	1 cup soup beans
1 pint green beans	1 pint lima beans
1 quart beef broth, OR 1 soup bone	1 pint tomatoes
1 pint peas	Water
2 tablespoons salt	½ cup rice

Chop the celery, carrots, cabbage and green beans finely. Combine them with the rest of the ingredients in water to cover (except the rice), and cook them for 2½ to 3 hours. Add the rice 15 minutes before serving.

Above: in wintry weather, travelers wrap themselves in wool or fur blankets to keep warm. Winter Vegetable Soup (facing page) has the same effect from the inside!

Corn Fritters

Ingredients

6 big ears of corn
2 eggs
½ teaspoon salt

Pepper to taste
1 cup flour
1 cup milk

Cut the corn with a salad cutter and add the rest of the ingredients. Mix it well and drop it by tablespoons into a frying pan with melted butter or lard.

Patches

Ingredients

6 medium-sized potatoes, raw
2 tablespoons flour
Milk

Salt and pepper
Parsley (optional)
Onions (optional)

Peel the potatoes, grind or grate them, and drain them in a colander. Stir in the flour and milk to make a thin batter, and add salt and pepper to taste. Parsley and onion may be added. Fry them in a well-oiled, hot skillet.

Dutch Slaw

Ingredients

1 large head cabbage, chopped
½ cup vinegar
1 cup celery, diced
2 teaspoons salt
½ teaspoon mustard seeds

½ cup chopped onions
2 cups sugar
1 green pepper, diced
1 teaspoon celery seeds

Mix together all the ingredients and put them into a glass jar. Screw on the lid, and refrigerate it until needed. It is ready to serve.

This salad will last a long time if refrigerated.

Above: two youths walk through the fields to a meeting of their "supper gang", one of the age group associations common in Amish society.

Three-Bean Salad

Ingredients

1 cup vinegar
1 cup sugar
2 tablespoons oil
Salt and pepper to taste
1 sweet onion, sliced
1 to 1¼ cups celery, diced

1 quart yellow beans, drained
1 quart green beans, drained
1 small can (1 pint) dark red kidney
   beans, washed and drained
1 green or red sweet pepper, sliced

Mix together the first 4 ingredients, then let the mixture stand while you slice the rest. Mix together all the vegetables, then add the vinegar mixture. Let it stand for 24 hours before serving.

Variations: Salad dressing may be used instead of the vinegar mixture.

Above: this benefit auction was for the Bareville Fire Co. With their
wooden barns and houses, fire protection is
particularly important to the Amish.

Little Beef Pies

Filling

1 beef bouillon cube
2 cups boiling water
3½ cups chopped cooked beef
2 teaspoons Worcestershire sauce
1½ teaspoons salt
1 teaspoon sugar

½ teaspoon paprika
¼ teaspoon pepper
1 package (10 ounces) frozen or
   canned mixed vegetables
¼ cup flour

Dissolve the bouillon cube in the boiling water and add the beef, Worcestershire sauce, salt, sugar, paprika and pepper. Add the vegetables, and cook the mixture for 5 minutes. Combine the flour with enough cold water to make a paste, and slowly stir it into the mixture, cooking it until it thickens. Then spoon it into 6 8-ounce oven-proof casseroles.

Pastry

1 cup flour
½ cup cornmeal
¾ teaspoon salt

⅓ cup shortening
4 tablespoons cold water

Make the pastry by sifting together the flour, cornmeal and salt. Cut in the shortening until the mixture resembles coarse crumbs. Sprinkle the water by tablespoons over the mixture. Stir it lightly with a fork until it is just damp. (If necessary, add another tablespoon of cold water to make the dough hold together.) Form the dough into a ball. Divide it into 6 parts and roll each part to form a circle large enough to fit the top of each casserole. Place the pastry circle over the filling, turn the edges under, and flute them. Make several cuts in the pastry to allow steam to escape. Bake the pies in a preheated oven at 450° for 12 to 15 minutes.

Above: horse-drawn buggies are slow-moving — an average
speed of 10 mph on a main route, slower up hills!

Savory Meat Loaf

Ingredients

1½ pounds ground beef, plus
   ½ pound ground pork, OR
   2 pounds ground beef
   (omit the pork)
¼ cup minced onions
1 cup oatmeal or crushed
   crackers

2½ teaspoons salt
1 beaten egg
¼ teaspoon pepper
1 teaspoon mustard
¼ cup ketchup
1 cup tomato juice
Bacon slices

Mix together the ingredients, then form the mixture into a loaf. Put a few bacon slices on top, and pour additional tomato juice over all. Bake the meat loaf at 350° to 375° for 1 hour.

Variations: The mixture may be pressed into a cake pan and topped with ketchup. Bake it for about 1 hour.

Try spreading a glaze over the loaf.

Glaze for Meat Loaf

½ cup brown sugar
1½ teaspoons prepared mustard

1 tablespoon Worcestershire sauce

Mix together the ingredients and add enough vinegar to make a paste. Spread the glaze over the meat loaf.

Above: this line of parked buggies indicates
a social gathering at the farmstead.

Busy Day Casserole

Ingredients

1½ cups cubed ham or hamburger
1 cup diced potatoes
1 cup diced carrots

½ cup peas, canned
½ cup green beans, canned

Brown the ham, then add the potatoes, carrots and water. Cook them until they are tender. Add the peas, beans and enough boiling water to cover them. Stir in 1 tablespoon of flour mixed with a little water. Put this mixture into a large casserole or small cake pan. Top it with your favorite biscuit dough (cheese may be added), dropped by tablespoons into the ham mixture. Bake the casserole at 350° for 20 to 30 minutes, or until done.

Schnitz und Knepp

Ingredients

1 quart dried apples (schnitz)
3 pounds ham
2 tablespoons brown sugar
2 cups flour
1 teaspoon salt

¼ teaspoon pepper
4 teaspoons baking powder
1 egg, well-beaten
Milk
3 tablespoons melted butter

Wash the dried apples then cover them with water to soak overnight. Cover the ham with boiling water and boil it for 3 hours. Add the apples and the water in which they were soaked and boil it for 1 hour longer. Add the sugar.

Make the dumplings by sifting together the flour, salt, pepper and baking powder. Stir in the beaten egg, milk (enough to make a fairly moist, stiff batter) and butter. Drop the batter by the tablespoon into the hot ham and apples. Cover it and cook it for 15 minutes. Serve it hot.

Spareribs and Sauerkraut

Ingredients

4 pounds or 2 sides spareribs
Salt and pepper
1 quart sauerkraut
1 apple, chopped

2 tablespoons brown sugar
1 tablespoon caraway seeds
1 onion, sliced
2 cups water

Cut the ribs and brown them in a skillet, adding seasonings. Pour off the fat. Place the sauerkraut mixed with the apple, sugar, caraway and onion in a kettle. Place the ribs on top. Pour the water around the meat and sauerkraut. Cover it tightly and simmer it for 1¼ to 1½ hours or until the ribs are very tender.

Baked Chicken

Ingredients

½ cup flour
2 teaspoons paprika
1 teaspoon pepper
¼ teaspoon dry mustard

3 teaspoons salt
1 cut up broiler or young chicken
¼ pound butter

Mix the dry ingredients well in a plastic bag, then coat the cut up chicken parts with the mixture. In a cake pan, melt the butter. Place the chicken parts in the pan, but do not crowd them. Bake the chicken at 350° for 1½ to 2 hours or until done.

Fried Salmon Patties

Ingredients

2 cups cracker crumbs
1 cup salmon
1 teaspoon salt (scant)

2 eggs, beaten
1½ cups milk
Pepper to taste

Roll the crackers until they are finely crushed. Mix them with the other ingredients. Drop the mixture by tablespoons and fry it with butter.

Above: time is of the essence when bringing in the hay,
so work continues as long as daylight allows.

Cornmeal Rolls

Ingredients

⅓ cup cornmeal
½ cup sugar
1 teaspoon salt
½ cup melted shortening
2 cups milk

2 eggs, beaten
1 package yeast
¼ cup lukewarm water
4 cups all-purpose flour

Combine the cornmeal, sugar, salt, shortening and milk in a double boiler, cooking the mixture until it is thick, stirring it often. Cool it to lukewarm, adding the eggs, and the yeast dissolved in water. Beat the mixture well. Let it rise in a greased bowl for 2 hours, then add the flour to form a soft dough. Knead it lightly, letting it rise in a greased bowl for 1 hour. Knead the dough again before rolling it out and cutting it with a biscuit cutter. Brush the dough pieces with fat, crease them, and fold them like Parkerhouse rolls. Place them on an oiled sheet to rise for 1 hour, then bake them at 375° for 15 minutes. This recipe makes a very soft dough. It yields 3 dozen rolls, which may be in different shapes — use flour generously when handling and shaping them.

Above: a team of mules pulls a motorized corn picker.

Delicious Pumpkin Bread

Ingredients

1⅔ cups sifted all-purpose flour
¼ teaspoon baking powder
1 teaspoon soda
¾ teaspoon salt
½ teaspoon cinnamon
½ teaspoon nutmeg
⅓ cup shortening

1⅓ cups sugar
½ teaspoon vanilla
2 eggs
1 cup mashed pumpkin
⅓ cup water
½ cup chopped walnuts or pecans

Grease a regular (9x5x3-inch) loaf pan. Sift together the flour, baking powder, soda, salt and spices. Cream the shortening, sugar and vanilla before adding the eggs, one at a time, and beating thoroughly after each addition. Stir in the pumpkin. Then add the previously sifted dry ingredients alternately with the water, beating just until the mixture is smooth. Be careful not to overbeat. Fold in the nuts. Turn the batter into the prepared pan and bake it at 350° for about 45 to 55 minutes or until done. Turn the bread out onto a wire rack and allow it to cool before storing it in a tight container. Slice and serve this bread with butter.

Above: a young boy holds onto his hat for a journey into
the non-Amish world outside the farmstead.

Pickled Beets

Ingredients

3 quarts small beets
3 cups vinegar
2 tablespoons salt

4 cups sugar
1½ cups water
2 cinnamon sticks (optional)

Cook the beets. Combine the rest of the ingredients and boil them to a syrup. Pour the boiling syrup over the beets in hot jars, then seal them. Cold pack them for 10 to 15 minutes.

Above: this Amish can cellar shows how housewives preserve their garden surplus for off-season use.

Tomato Pepper Relish

Ingredients
½ peck green tomatoes
8 red peppers

2 or more large onions

Put the above ingredients through a food chopper. Boil them for 15 minutes, then remove them from the heat and add salt. Boil them again for 15 minutes. Drain them through a colander, then add the following ingredients.

1 pint vinegar
1 pint sugar
2 sticks cinnamon

2 tablespoons allspice
2 tablespoons whole cloves

Boil the mixture rapidly, then add 1 tablespoon of celery seeds and 1 teaspoon of mustard seeds. Jar and seal.

Above: the red warning triangle and wing mirror on this buggy
are concessions to traveling in modern traffic.

Griddle Cakes

Ingredients

1⅓ cups all-purpose flour
2 tablespoons sugar
3 teaspoons baking powder
3 tablespoons melted shortening
   or oil

1 egg
¾ teaspoon salt
1¼ cups milk

Combine all the ingredients and mix them well. Lightly grease a skillet for the first griddle cakes only. Fry them until they are puffy and bubbly, turning to brown the other side. Then serve them hot with butter and maple syrup. This recipe yields ten 6-inch griddle cakes.

Above: preserves, cheese, sausages and bread, this wholesome
and appetizing spread is entirely home-made.

Raisin Oatmeal Batter Bread

Ingredients

1 package active dry yeast
2 cups warm water
1½ teaspoons salt
3 tablespoons sugar
2 tablespoons soft shortening

2 cups all-purpose flour
2 cups whole wheat flour
1 cup rolled oats
½ cup seedless raisins

In a large mixing bowl, dissolve the yeast in the warm water. Stir in the salt, sugar and shortening, plus 2 cups of the flour, and the rolled oats. Beat this mixture for 3 minutes, then stir in the rest of the flour and the raisins, mixing it until the batter is smooth and satiny. Cover it with a cloth and let it rise in a warm place until it is double in size. Stir it down while counting slowly to 15, then spoon the batter into a greased loaf pan. Cover it with a cloth and let it rise before baking it in 2 greased loaf pans at 350° for 50 minutes.

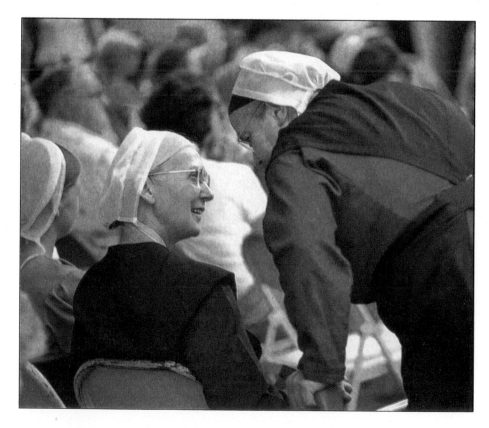

Above: dress is strictly regulated. These women are wearing the long-sleeved dress, black apron and pointed cape appropriate for older married women in Lancaster County.

Fresh Blueberry Cake

Ingredients

½ cup butter or margarine
1 cup sugar
2 eggs
2 cups all-purpose flour

½ teaspoon salt
3 teaspoons baking powder
1 cup milk
1 cup blueberries

Cream the butter or margarine, then add the sugar a little at a time, and cream it again. Add the eggs and some of the flour, sifted with the salt and baking powder. Blend this slowly, adding the milk and the rest of the flour. Wash the berries, dry them on a towel, then dust them with some flour. Add them to the batter just before baking. Pour the batter into a greased and floured pan, 9x13x2 inches. Sprinkle it with cinnamon and sugar, nutmeg, cloves or whatever appeals to you. Bake it at 325° for 45 minutes. Serve the cake with whipped cream or ice cream.

Variations: If blueberries are scarce, raisins or currants can be substituted.

Above: used for receiving company, the parlor is more elaborately furnished and decorated than other rooms in an Amish house.

Apple Fritters

Ingredients

1 cup flour
2 tablespoons sugar
½ cup milk
1½ teaspoons baking powder

½ teaspoon salt
1 egg
5 or 6 apples
Icing sugar, or syrup

Make a batter by combining the flour, sugar, milk, baking powder, salt and egg. Cover and peel the apples, then slice them and put them into the batter. Drop them by spoonfuls into 1 inch of fat or oil in a frying pan. Test the apples with a fork — they are done when soft. Drain them on paper towels or in a colander. Sprinkle the fritters with icing sugar or eat them with syrup. This recipe makes about 4 skillets full.

Facing page: delicious Apple Fritters might be the reward for helping to pick the family's store of apples which will then be cooked, canned or preserved in a variety of ways.

Apple-Cranberry Dumplings

Syrup

2 cups water
2 cups sugar
½ teaspoon cinnamon

½ teaspoon cloves
½ cup butter

Combine the first 4 ingredients and boil the mixture for 5 minutes. Remove this syrup from the heat and add the butter.

Biscuit Dough

2 cups all-purpose flour, sifted
1 teaspoon salt
1 tablespoon baking powder

2 tablespoons sugar
½ cup shortening
¾ cup milk

Sift together the dry ingredients and cut in the shortening. Gradually add the milk, tossing the mixture to make a soft dough. Roll it out on a floured board to form an 18x12-inch rectangle.

Filling

4 cups grated, peeled apples
1 cup cooked, drained whole
    cranberries, OR 1 cup whole
    cranberry sauce

½ cup black walnuts, chopped

Spread the dough with the apples, cranberries and nuts. Roll it up like a jelly roll and cut it into 1-inch slices. Place them in a 13x9x2-inch pan. Pour the hot syrup over all and bake them in a hot oven (425°) for 40 minutes. Serve the dumplings warm.

Above: fertilizing is done according to the soil's needs,
the machine pulled by horses, naturally.

Baked Berry Pudding

Ingredients

1 tablespoon butter
½ cup milk
1 teaspoon baking powder
½ cup sugar

1 cup all-purpose flour
1 cup sweetened berries
1 cup boiling water

Mix together the butter, milk, baking powder, sugar and flour to make a dough, then spread it in a greased, deep baking dish. Pour the berries and boiling water over the dough, and bake it at 400° until the cake part is done.

Lemon Pie

Ingredients

3 tablespoons cornstarch
1½ cups sugar
Juice and grated rind of 1 lemon

3 eggs, separated
1¼ cups boiling water
6 tablespoons sugar

Mix together the cornstarch, 1½ cups of sugar, and lemon juice. Add the beaten egg yolks followed by the water in which the lemon rind has been boiled. (Discard the rind.) Cook this in a double boiler, then pour it into a baked pie crust. Beat the egg whites until they are stiff with the 6 tablespoons of sugar before spreading this mixture over the pie. Brown it in the oven.

Paper Bag Apple Pie

Filling

6 cups coarsely sliced or chopped
    apples
½ cup sugar

2 tablespoons flour
½ teaspoon nutmeg
2 tablespoons lemon juice

Measure the apples into a bowl, and mix them with the sugar, flour, nutmeg and lemon juice. Turn them into an unbaked pie shell and pat them down evenly.

Topping

½ cup butter
½ cup flour

½ cup brown or white sugar

Measure out the butter, flour and sugar, cutting in the butter with a pastry blender until crumbs are the size of peas. Sprinkle this evenly over the apples and pat it down around the edges. Slide the pie into a brown paper bag and fold the end under the pie. Put it onto a cookie sheet for easy handling. Bake it at 425° for 50 minutes.

The benefit of this method is a pie with no scorched rim, no under-baked apples, no boiling over in your clean oven, and no grief in general!

Above: even the horses and mules are allowed to rest on Sundays,
when only essential work, such as milking the cows, is done.

Peach Crumb Pie

Ingredients

2½ tablespoons tapioca
¾ cup sugar
¼ teaspoon salt
4 cups sliced peaches

⅓ cup packed brown sugar
¼ cup flour
½ teaspoon cinnamon
2½ tablespoons soft butter

Mix together the first 4 ingredients, then let the mixture set for 5 minutes before pouring it into an unbaked 9-inch pie shell. Mix the rest of the ingredients for the crumb topping, then put it on top of the fruit filling. Bake the pie at 425° for 45 to 50 minutes.

Variations: Other fruit may be used, but this recipe is especially good with apples.

Above: monthly sewing circles give women the opportunity to socialize, to quilt and to sew items for relief and benefit auctions.

Shoo-Fly Pie

Ingredients

2 cups molasses
2 cups hot water
1 cup light brown sugar
1 teaspoon soda (scant)
5 cups all-purpose flour

2 cups light brown sugar
1 cup shortening (scant)
½ teaspoon soda
½ teaspoon cream of tartar

To make the syrup, mix together the first 4 ingredients until they are dissolved. (Use 1 cup or more of syrup per 9-inch pie shell.) Then mix the remaining ingredients to crumb consistency. Pour the syrup into unbaked pie crusts and divide the crumbs over top. Bake them for 10 minutes at 450°, for 30 minutes more at 375°, then for 30 minutes longer at 350°. This recipe makes 4 pies.

Variations: Try adding 2 teaspoons of nutmeg and 3 teaspoons of cinnamon to the crumbs.

Lemon Sauce for Shoo-Fly Pie

2 tablespoons cornstarch
½ cup sugar
¼ teaspoon salt
2 cups boiling water

¼ cup butter or margarine
3 teaspoons lemon juice
1 tablespoon grated lemon rind

Mix together in a saucepan the cornstarch, sugar and salt. Gradually stir in the boiling water. Cook the mixture, stirring it constantly, until it boils and becomes thick and clear. Remove it from the heat, and stir in the remaining ingredients. Serve this sauce warm over Shoo-Fly Pie. This recipe yields 2¼ cups of sauce.

Above: dressed like miniature versions of their parents,
these children set off for school together.

Strawberry Pie

Ingredients

1½ quarts fresh strawberries
2 cups sugar

½ cup cornstarch

Combine the strawberries and sugar and let them stand for 2 hours. Drain off the juice and add water to make 2 cups. Blend in the cornstarch and cook it over low heat until it has thickened. Mix it with the strawberries, then let it cool. Put it into a baked pie crust or graham cracker crust and serve it with whipped cream.

Above: the family produce garden is edged with rows of flowers,
which are weeded using a hand cultivator.

Lemon Crisps

Ingredients

1¾ cups shortening
1 cup granulated sugar
1 cup brown sugar
2 tablespoons lemon juice
2 eggs

2 teaspoons grated lemon rind
5½ cups all-purpose flour
½ teaspoon salt
½ teaspoon soda

Mix the ingredients together well, then form the dough into small balls. Place them on a cookie sheet and flatten them. Bake the cookies at 350° for 10 to 12 minutes.

Orange Crisps: Substitute orange juice and rind for the lemons.

Above: some Amish who do not farm engage
in carriage repair and building.

Old-Fashioned Ginger Cookies

Ingredients

3 cups baking molasses
1 cup sugar
2 cups shortening
10 cups flour (5 cups pastry,
    5 cups bread)

1 teaspoon salt
2 tablespoons soda
1 to 2 tablespoons ginger
1 teaspoon cinnamon
2 cups sour milk or buttermilk

Heat together the molasses and sugar, add the shortening and stir the mixture until it is smooth. Remove it from the heat. Sift together the dry ingredients and add this mixture alternately with the sour milk. Stir it to make a smooth dough, then work it with your hands for 5 minutes. Chill the dough and roll it out to ½-inch thickness. Cut it into cookies, and glaze them with a beaten egg. Bake them at 350° for 20 to 25 minutes. This recipe makes 8 dozen cookies.

Above: these thoughtfully picked flowers may be to decorate
the parlor in anticipation of a weekend visit.

Fresh Strawberry Jam

Ingredients
3 cups strawberries, well crushed
6 cups sugar

1 package Certo crystals
1 cup water

Mix the strawberries and sugar together and let the mixture stand for 20 minutes. Stir it several times. Combine the Certo crystals and water. Boil this for 1 minute stirring constantly. Mix it with the berries and stir it for 2 minutes. Put it into jars and cold pack them a few minutes to seal them. Store them in the freezer.

Variations: Other fruit may be used instead of strawberries.

Above: celosia flowers rim a vegetable garden
with vibrant reds and yellows.

Simple Apple Butter

Ingredients
4 gallons apples, unpeeled,
   quartered

1 gallon corn syrup
6 pounds sugar

Put the apples into a heavy kettle or canner with a tight-fitting lid. Pour the syrup and sugar over the apples and let them set overnight to form juice. Bring the mixture to a slow boil and cook it, covered, for 3 hours. Do not open the lid or stir the mixture during the entire cooking period. Put it through a strainer.

Cider Apple Butter
3 gallons schnitz (dried apple pieces)
1 gallon sweet cider

½ gallon corn syrup
4 pounds sugar

Follow the directions above.

Above: Ephrata Cloister is a Protestant communal society established in 1732. The simple lifestyle of Cloister sisters is epitomized by this picture.